ribbonrie

Scrapbooking :: Cardmaking :: Home Décor :: Gifts

© 2005 Making Memories®

Published and Created by Making Memories®
Executive Director: Paula Chen Su
Creative Director of Publications: Gail Pierce-Watne
Associate Editor: Jayme Shepherd
Art Director: Kevin Thompson
Designer: Doug Seely
Writer: Jennifer Kofford
Photographer: Skylar Nielsen
Photographer's Assistant: Angie Hancock

For information about bulk sales or promotional pricing, please contact Customer Service at 1.800.286.5263 or customerservice@makingmemories.com.

Printed in the USA.
ISBN 1-893352-16-1

contents

all about ribbon

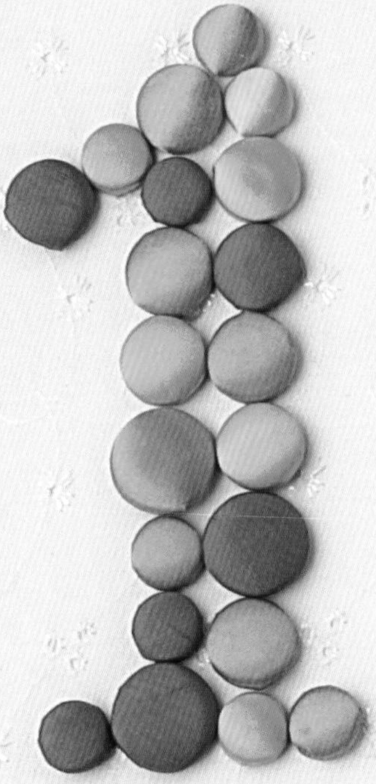

RIBBON

In the simplest terms, ribbon is a narrow strip or band of fabric finished at the edges and used for tying, trimming and finishing. But that's just the beginning of this most versatile and varied embellishment. In this book, we've set out not only to explore the wonderful world of ribbon but also to push its limits. We hope you're inspired and enlightened as we introduce you to the numerous ways to incorporate ribbon into everyday living and the most special of occasions. Enjoy!

all about ribbon

types of RIBBON

Ribbon is available in thousands of colors, textures, widths and types. Search ribbon and trimming stores, craft stores and online merchants to find just the right one for your project. With as many choices as there are out there, we're sure you'll find exactly what you're looking for.

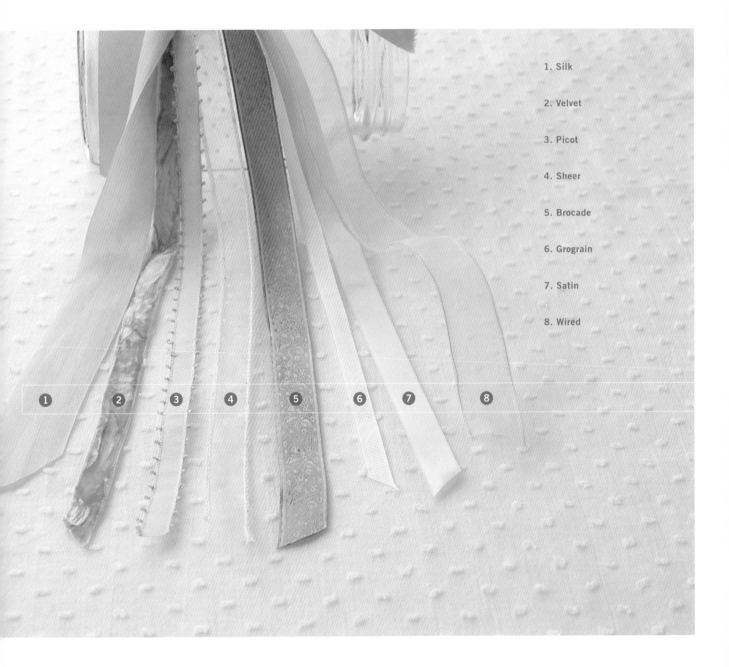

1. Silk

2. Velvet

3. Picot

4. Sheer

5. Brocade

6. Grograin

7. Satin

8. Wired

finishing ends OF RIBBON

The ends of your ribbons can become a design element on your project themselves. Make them match the mood or style of your piece and you've got magic. Following are just a few of the many ways for cutting or finishing ends. You may want to consider using a fray retardant like Fray-Check or a craft glue that dries clear when appropriate.

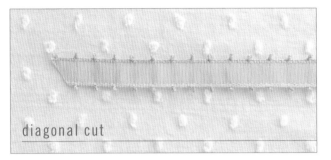

diagonal cut

Clip end at a diagonal in the desired direction.

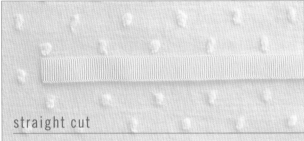

straight cut

Clip straight across ribbon.

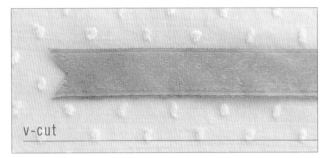

v-cut

Fold ribbon in half lengthwise, lining up edges. Clip end in a diagonal from the fold to the edges and unfold.

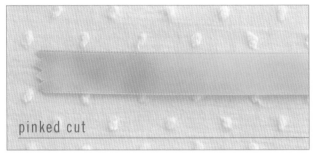

pinked cut

Use sharp pinking shears to cut end or clip several small notches across end using sharp scissors.

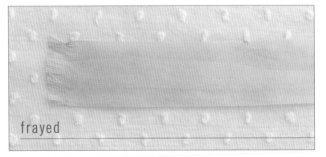

frayed

Pull ribbon along edge of cut to loosen fibers. Remove threads until end is frayed as desired.

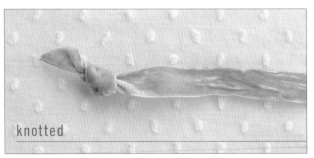

knotted

Tie a knot at the end of your ribbon and trim excess if necessary.

gathering and PLEATING RIBBON

For the ultimate decorative detail, nothing beats gathers and pleats. They're definitely feminine but can even be surprisingly masculine. It all depends on the type and style of ribbon you choose. Here are a few techniques that'll help you start puckering and pulling.

1. Zigzag Gather: Hand stitch a running stitch in a zigzag pattern along the length of ribbon. Loop thread over the top and through the back each time zigzag reaches an edge. Pull thread to create a puffy S-shaped gather.

2. Stapled Pleat: Fold pleats along the length of ribbon, stapling each to secure.

3. Knife Pleat with Side Stitching: Fold pleats along length of ribbon, pinning or basting each as you go. Machine stitch along the bottom edge with a matching or contrasting thread. Layer a decorative ribbon along bottom edge to cover stitching if desired.

4. Knife Pleat with Center Stitching: Repeat same process as Side Stitching but machine stitch down the center of the ribbon.

5. Simple Gather: Machine stitch or hand stitch along center of ribbon with a long stitch. Pull one end of threads to gather. Stitch along both edges for a different gathered look or use elastic thread in the bobbin for stretchy gathered ribbon.

6. Tight and Twisted Gather: Machine stitch or hand stitch along center of ribbon with a tight stitch to tightly gather a narrow piece of ribbon, causing it to twist.

7. Embellished Gather: Follow the Simple Gather process with hand stitching, adding beads to stitches as you go. Experiment with other embellishments for a variety of looks.

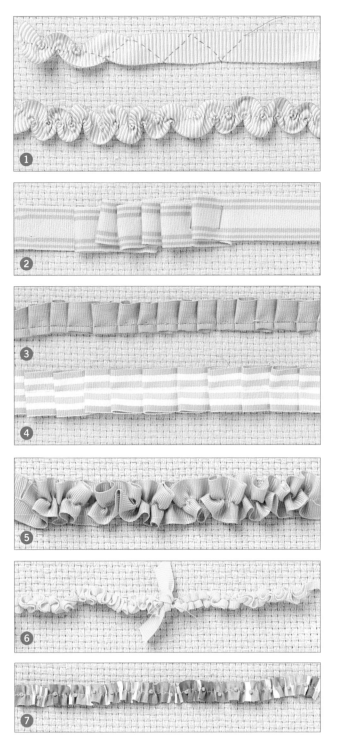

While ribbon is stunning on its own, you can make it uniquely yours by adding journaling, titles, quotes or other meaningful words. There are several ways to do it—choose the best technique for your project and you'll get instant impact.

printing on RIBBON

1. Computer Printing: Type desired text onto screen, format to landscape setting and print onto paper. Adhere ribbon over printed text with spray adhesive and run through printer again. Ribbon should be going into printer end first. Text will print onto ribbon. Remove carefully from paper.

2. Clear Stickers: Carefully remove sticker from backing, position over ribbon where desired and apply. Rub thoroughly with a bone folder to adhere completely and trim edges if necessary.

3. Rub-Ons: Follow package directions to carefully apply rub-on to ribbon. Rub-ons are available in a wide variety of colors, styles and sizes and will adhere to nearly every type of ribbon.

4. Stamping: Use foam or rubber stamps with paint and stamping ink to stamp onto ribbon. Let dry completely. For best results, use a permanent ink that won't smear.

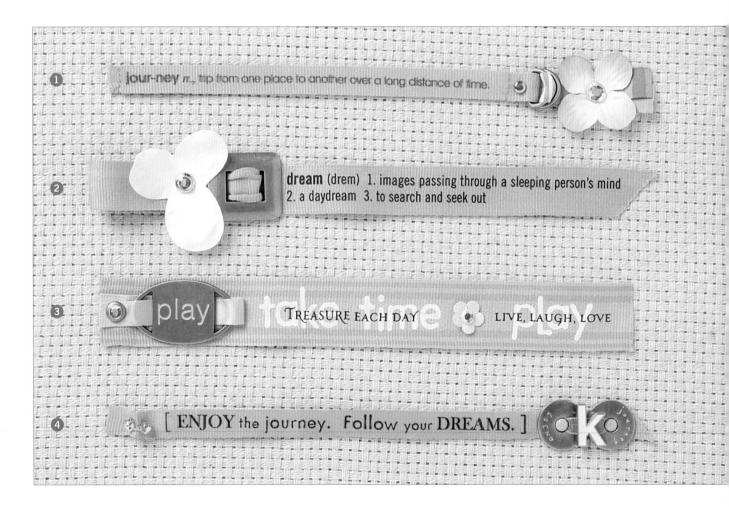

RIBBON *flowers*

Flowers are one of the hottest embellishments in crafting and there are many ways to create them from a simple length of ribbon. Try these techniques for creating your own garden of custom blooms keeping a few hints in mind:

1. Flower size will vary depending on the length and width of the ribbon you choose.
2. Begin each flower with an extra stitch to prevent thread from pulling through ribbon.
3. When necessary, double-thread the needle to prevent breakage when gathering.

1. Twisted Petals: Twist the center of a 2¼-inch strip of ribbon and fold in half to create a petal. Repeat until desired number of petals is created. Stitch petals with a long thread and pull tightly into a circle to form flower. Add more stitches to anchor petals together and tuck raw edges through center. Layer two sets of petals together and stitch together to form a double flower.

2. Pulled Thread Flowers: Stitch a long running stitch along the back of a long length of ribbon. Stitches should be about 1½ inches long with a tiny stitch in between. Fold ribbon in half and, while holding the ends together, pull on both threads at the same time to gather petals. When gathered, tightly tie thread in the back of the flower.

3. Single and Double Rosettes: Stitch a running stitch along the edge of a strip of ribbon curving upward at each end. Pull to gather as you go. A longer strip will create a double rosette, a shorter strip a single. Pull gathers tight, secure with a few stitches and trim excess. Form into a flower and stitch together, tucking the raw edges to the back.

4. Gathered Rose: Tie a knot at one end of a length of ribbon. Starting at the knot, stitch a running stitch along one edge, pulling as you go. When flower is as desired, finish with an upward curve to the opposite edge and trim excess ribbon. Gather tightly, wrap around the knot and tightly wrap with thread. Secure well with a few stitches.

5. Rickrack: Count 16 points along bottom edge of rickrack and cut. With double-threaded needle, stitch through the 16 points and pull on end of thread to gather. Make sure petals all go in the same direction. Pull tight, tie ends of thread together to secure and glue ends of rickrack together.

Tassels are a quick way to add a touch of class to a wide range of projects. Experiment with mixing and matching types and textures of ribbon to create a truly custom trimming. They're simple to make when you follow these steps.

6. Gathered Petals: Stitch a running stitch along the edge of a length of ribbon, curving upward three, four or five times depending on desired number of petals. Pull thread to gather, form flower and stitch through center several times to secure.

7. Cut Petals: Fold a small length of ribbon and cut a petal shape on the fold. Unfold to create two petals. Repeat until desired number of petals is cut. Layer to form a flower and anchor with a few stitches in the center. Pinch the center and stitch in a tuck or two through the back to give the flower dimension. Add embellishment for center.

1. Wrapped Tassels: To create tassels that are 3 inches long, start with 2 to 3 yards of narrow ribbon or rickrack. The length will determine fullness of tassel. Loosely wrap ribbon around a 3-inch piece of cardboard. Use a strand of coordinating ribbon to tie through the loops of one end and carefully slip tassel off cardboard. Wind another piece of ribbon around the tassel just below the top, tie tightly and stitch to secure. Trim ends if necessary. Leave tassel looped or cut to fringe. Length of tassel can vary depending on size of cardboard piece and length of ribbon.

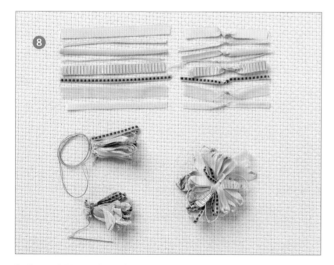

8. Knotted Bloom: Cut four 4-inch strips from eight different narrow ribbons. Tie a knot in the center of each and fold in half to form petals. Using a doubled thread, stitch through the ends to form a long strand of petals. When complete, gather tightly and roll to form a flower. Wind the remaining thread around the base of the flower and stitch to secure.

RIBBON *storage*

A growing collection of spools and strips can easily and quickly get out of control. The key for keeping things tidy is a manageable and maintainable storage system. Here are a few ideas for reigning in your ribbon.

1. Jars and Shelf: Hang a simple store-bought shelf above your workspace and line with ribbon-filled glass jars. Organize by type, color or in the most aesthetically pleasing arrangement. You'll be able to quickly spot what you're looking for all while making a great style statement.

2. Hooks and Book Rings: Place ribbon in resealable baggies, punch a hole in each one and thread onto book rings. Organized by color, width or type, you'll be able to quickly flip through the baggies until you find what you need. Hang rings from hooks for accessible vertical storage.

3. Custom Mini-Binder: For the crafter, scrapbooker or cardmaker on-the-go, storage solutions for traveling from one place to another are essential. This little binder, rings and is perfect for assembling a custom assortment of ribbon for your crop or craft night. Just throw it in a bag and hit the road.

layering

monograms

distressing

accents

attachments

tying accents

knots   backgrounds

borders

flowers   hinges

Esther Howland is known as the "Mother of the Valentine". In the mid 1800's, she started creating fancy handmade cards decorated with lace, ribbons and colorful pictures known as "scrap". And the rest, as they say, is history. Never before has cardmaking been more popular and, in the spirit of Esther, we've created gorgeous cards using many of the same embellishments she did. Make a few of these cards and you'll make Esther proud.

Flower Card
By Maggie Holmes

how to: Cut several flowers in graduating sizes from fabric and tulle. Layer together, top with strips of folded MM Kids Trim, attach through with a Crystal Brad and attach to front of card. Thread ribbon through holes to attach base to insert.

intricate layering fabric and ribbon

moderate

simple

how to: Fold two strips of MM Kids Trim, place under several graduating sizes of Petals and a small flower cut from trim. Attach through front flap of card with a Crystal Brad. Thread ribbon through holes to attach base to insert.

how to: Fold a strip of MM Kids Trim, layer under two Blossoms and attach all layers with mini brad to front flap of card. Thread ribbon through holes to attach base to insert.

how to start

THREADED CLOSURE TECHNIQUE
1. Thread both ends of a ribbon strip through punched holes on the front of piece.
2. Pull ribbon to center.
3. Cross ribbon ends on back and thread back up through opposite holes.

RIBBON
roses

Our Sincere Thanks
By Lynne Montgomery

how to: Create rose by rolling and flattening a wide ribbon. Tuck the end of a thin ribbon under flower and lay flat to create stem. At the bottom, loop ribbon up and around to create a leaf. Place a small strip of ribbon behind window so that the edge is visible when card is closed.

our
sincere
thanks

RIBBON
monograms

Don't have a lot of time and still want the classic look of the ribbon monogram cards? Simply skip the embossing step and you'll still create a card that'll turn heads.

Forever
By Loni Stevens

how to: Trace letter in the square on the front of card and punch holes at intersecting lines. Thread ribbon through holes in a backstitch fashion to form the letter "F".

Friendship Card Set and Box

By Charla Campbell

how to: Cut the outside cover of a box from chipboard, including enough for a ½-inch spine. Cover inside and outside with fabric, add embellishments and ribbon closure. Paint a small box lid to match, cover inside with fabric and attach inside chipboard cover. Customize note cards and envelopes with ribbon, foam stamps and paint and place inside.

combining ribbon AND FABRIC

slimming ribbon AND FABRIC

soul mates

forever

for always and endlessly, forever now

Happy Anniversary
By Charla Campbell

how to: Adhere two coordinating fabrics to front and flap of card. Place ribbon under flap, lining up right edge and leaving a slight overlap on the left side. Stitch to secure. Punch three holes in right edge of insert and tie three coordinating ribbons through.

the final touch

*ribbon*CLOSURES

Card File

By Janet Hopkins

how to: Cut cardstock to size and fold to create covers of card file. Adhere vellum envelopes inside along the fold and add tabs along openings. Use rub-ons to label each envelope. Create cards using ribbon, rub-ons and other embellishments and file according to theme. Use wide ribbon and Ribbon Attachments to create a belt-like closure for the outside.

card
file

thanks.

couldn't do
it without
you!

ribbon ACCENTS

how to start

ALTERNATING STRIPES TECHNIQUE
1. Choose a striped ribbon.
2. Cut several small pieces of the same ribbon
   and wrap around a long piece.
3. Secure strips on the back with adhesive. When
   complete, effect will be alternating horizontal
   and vertical stripes.
4. Wrap long ribbon strip around card, scrapbook
   page or other project.

simple

simple

Baby By Wendy Anderson

how to: Trim MM Kids Paper to fit flap on front of card base. Create flower from felt and place in upper left corner. Twist two strips of ribbon and tuck under either side of flower to create leaves.

Baby Girl By Kris Stanger

how to: Adhere ribbon diagonally across front flap of card. Adhere ribbon diagonally in opposite direction to create a French ribbon board effect. Clip phrases from Ribbon Words and attach under flower.

change it up

Weaving the entire front of a card can be time consuming. If you're not quite ready to dive in yet, try just one or two rows across the top, bottom or middle. It's also a great solution when you want to create a card in a hurry.

Adore You By Julie Turner

how to: Choose and lay several ribbons across the front of a card. Mark and cut five rows of vertical slits across the card at even intervals and weave ribbons through. Add embellishments and greeting in bottom right corner.

*weaving*RIBBON

RIBBON *flowers*

Friendship

By Loni Stevens

how to: Turn gatefold card base on its side and stitch around bottom flap to create pocket. Attach MM Kids Trim along edge of top flap by stitching down the middle and add rub-ons to finish front of card. Loop a length of ribbon to create flower petals and attach to insert. Stitch rickrack to create stem.

You Are My Favorite
By Jennifer Jensen

how to: Thread ribbon onto needle and backstitch around window opening of card. Apply rub-ons to ribbon to create greeting. Adhere Avenue Embellishment paper inside card, leaving a slight overhang on the right side so that it is visible when card is closed.

Forever
By Jennifer Jensen

how to: Cut six strips of ribbon, divide into pairs and create interlocking ribbons. Place each pair across bottom of pocket card base and either secure on the back or through slits cut in the sides. Add a strip of coordinating patterned paper in the middle of the ribbon.

ribbon borders AND TYING

simple

how to start

INTERLOCKING RIBBON TECHNIQUE
1. Cut two strips of ribbon about an inch longer than the piece you want to embellish.
2. Fold one strip in half and pass the second ribbon through the loop.
3. Fold second ribbon in half so that ribbons interlock.
4. Lay across card, page or project and adhere on the back.

weaving RIBBON

When you want to add a little extra something, do a tight zigzag stitch around the edge of the insert. It'll add texture and color with minimal effort.

Missing You
By Mellette Berezoski

how to: Place a setting mat inside the card pocket. Using a craft knife, cut evenly-spaced slits through the striped flap of the card. Remove the mat and weave ribbon through the slits, wrapping around the back and tying a bow where the ends meet.

Thanks By Janet Hopkins

how to: Layer and overlap several strips of Avenue Embellishment paper on the front of the card. Tie strips of ribbon around some of the paper strips. Stitch several short vertical lines along paper to secure.

Celebrate By Wendy Anderson

how to: Thread a Ribbon Charm onto a strip of Ribbon Words. String Ribbon Charm Alphabet letters on ribbon and tie a knot at either end of word to keep letters in place. Wrap both embellished ribbons around card base, securing on back. Add another small strip of ribbon to upper left corner and attach painted Gameboard Shape on top.

moderate

simple

tying RIBBON

RIBBON BORDER *accents*

Little Man

By Charla Campbell

how to: Adhere patterned paper to left flap of card and paint circles on right flap using a pencil eraser. Fold and staple or tie and staple strips of ribbon to top left edge to create the look of fringe.

the final touch

Happy Birthday

By Joanna Bolick

how to: Tie knots in the ends of ribbon strips, pull through holes in front of bookplate and adhere ends on the back. Trim ends on front if necessary. Attach bookplate to front of card and add other embellishments.

Thanks

By Erin Terrell

how to: Wrap two coordinating colors of Ribbon Words around the opening and edge of the card, knotting the bottom one on the front. Adhere a strip of ribbon across bottom to cover paper seam.

RIBBON *knots*

ribbon BACKGROUNDS

Congrats
By Maggie Holmes

how to: Create gatefold card out of cardstock, cut strips of MM Kids Paper and attach across middle. Adhere and stitch several coordinating strips of ribbon across front and attach buttons, using a strip of ribbon as a closure.

another look

congrats! You did it...
nice job

RIBBON
borders

Happy Birthday
By Erin Terrell

how to: Create a border around the outside of the
card by laying and adhering strips of ribbon about
½ inch in from edges. Trim ends to fit card.

knotting
RIBBON

Love
By Mellette Berezoski

how to: Draw heart design on front of card with pencil. Tie various ribbons into knots, trim, and adhere to completely cover pencil design. Interlock several ribbons and wrap around bottom edge.

how to start

TINY KNOTS TECHNIQUE
1. Choose a variety of ribbon in similar widths.
2. Cut ribbon into strips of equal lengths.
3. Tie knots into each strip and pull tight.
4. Trim ends close to knot and adhere in desired shape.

RIBBON *flowers*

Thank You
By Mellette Berezoski

how to: Stitch several angled lines up the card base to create a stem. Loop and twist ribbon to create petals of flower and tack down with a few stitches using a needle and thread. Pierce two holes to the left side of stem and thread ribbon through to create leaf.

THANK YOU

ribbon
HINGES

For Keeps By Wendy Anderson

how to: Cut cardstock to create four
pieces of equal size. Punch three holes
along edges of each piece. Tie pieces
together with small strips of ribbon to
create an accordion-style card. Add
greeting and embellishments as desired.

another look

mixing and
MATCHING RIBBON

moderate

Happy Birthday

By Jennifer Jensen

how to: Overlap edges of several ribbon strips and stitch together to attach. Tuck right side of stacked ribbon under window opening and pull through so that ends of ribbon slightly extend beyond right edge of card and attach.

XoXo
By Jennifer Jensen

how to: Staple two small strips of Vintage Hip Trim to top of printed and inked tag. Pass several long strips of ribbon through the button shank, glue button to striped section of pocket and arrange ends of ribbon as desired.

Happy Birthday

XoXo

simple

tags & wrapping

RIBBON

tying

wrapping

handles

accents

bows

The Chinese started doing it in 105 A.D., the Egyptians in 800 A.D. and the Europeans in 1085. We're talking, of course, about wrapping gifts. Ever since paper was invented, gift giving has been as much about the presentation as about the gift itself. And when you combine the right wrapping with the right ribbon, you've got magic. Make that first impression count with the gift wrapping ideas you'll find in the following pages.

tags & wrapping

ribbon tying
intricate

Floral Gift Bag By Mellette Berezoski

how to: Cut two 6x12-inch rectangles. Score and fold in ½-inch along
one of the long ends of each piece and adhere with double-sided tape. Score
and fold in 1-inch along the other long end of each piece. With a coordinating
patterned paper, cut two 2x12-inch strips. Score and fold in ½-inch along one of the
short ends of each piece and tape. Score and fold in 6 inches from the other short end of each
piece. Arrange pieces so that rectangles are front and back panels and strips are side panels. Mark
along corners, set eyelets and tie all pieces together with strips of ribbon. Tape folded-in pieces together to
create bottom panel. Set eyelets along the top edges of front and back panels and tie rope through for handles.

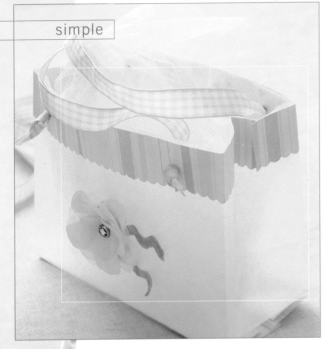

simple

moderate

how to: Cut top off store-bought gift bag. Cut patterned paper to 1½-inch strips and trim with decorative scissors across bottom edge. Adhere strips around top of bag and punch four small holes in the top for handles. Thread ribbon handles through the holes, tying knots to secure. Create layered flower using Petals, add rickrack underneath for leaves and attach to bag with brad.

how to: Cut top off store-bought gift bag. Cut patterned paper to 1½-inch strips and trim with decorative scissors across bottom edge. Adhere strips around top of bag, punch four small holes in the top for handles and set eyelets. Thread ribbon through holes and secure with mini brads to create handles. Adhere bows and attach to sides, tie strips of ribbon around Monogram and adhere to front.

the final touch

ribbon
ACCENTS

Travel Box

By Maggie Holmes

how to: Prime and paint metal box. Wrap ribbon across and around lid and secure ends. Wrap the first letter of the title completely with Ribbon Words and paint a variety of Jigsaw Alphabet and Gameboard Alphabet letters to complete the title. Tie or staple strips of ribbon on some of the letters. Tie various strips of ribbon to cover the handle and trim. Staple three Gameboard Tags together, add Metal Signage and fold two ribbon tabs under the edge.

WRAPPING STENCIL TECHNIQUE

1. Cut strips of ribbon slightly longer than width of stencil.
2. Starting along sides of letter, begin wrapping strips and adhering on back.
3. Work toward top and bottom, continuing to wrap and overlapping where necessary until stencil is completely covered.

how to start

wrapping WITH RIBBON

Best Buds Gift Box

By Hillary Bevan

how to: Wrap two lengths of MM Kids Trim both vertically and horizontally around wrapped box and secure ends on the back. Where ribbons intersect on the top, tie them together with a small piece of string, knot and trim. Thread Stitches through button holes, knot, trim and adhere over string. Add a sanded Gameboard Tag under one of the buttons and attach a Page Pebble on top.

[this is your special day.]

[treat yourself to something fun.]

[celebrate.]

Happy Birthday Gift Bag
By Loni Stevens

how to: Cut a 7x17-inch rectangle from canvas. Fold the short ends in ½-inch and pin. Cut two strips of Woven Ribbon to the desired handle length and pin to inside of short ends. Stitch and remove pins. Pass one short and one long length of ribbon through both sides of a ribbon slide and tack down ends. Use iron-on adhesive to adhere to the right side of the bag 1½ inches down from one of the short ends. Fold bag in half, right sides together and stitch along edges leaving a ½-inch seam allowance. Turn bag right side out, stamp greeting on front and iron on additional text using t-shirt transfer.

ribbon HANDLES

ribbon ACCENTS

shining with light 2. bright
vivid 3. lively and cheer

Fabric-Covered Tag

By Charla Campbell

how to: Cover tag with fabric and trim to fit. Tie a strip of ribbon around a corsage pin, dangle a charm from knot with a jump ring and pass through tag to attach.

Instead of covering a tag with fabric, try covering one with wrapped ribbon. Mix a variety of complementary colors, textures and widths. It's a great look and a great way to use your leftover scraps.

change it up

*ribbon*BOWS

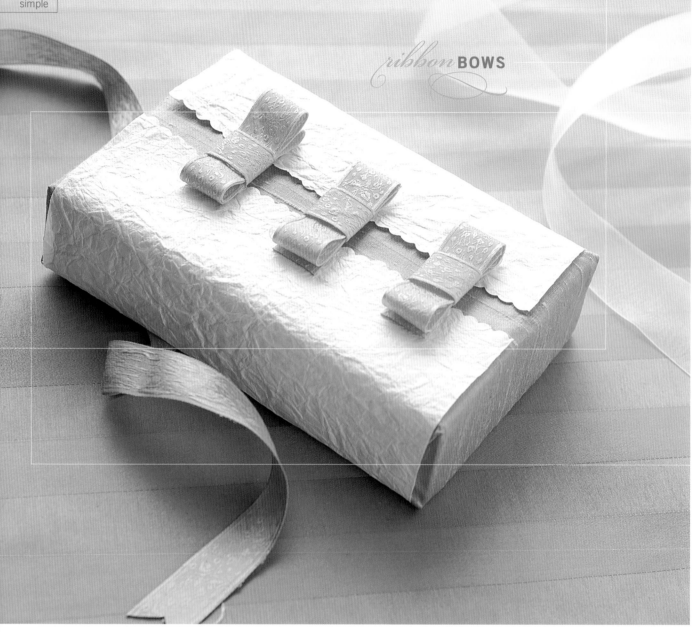

Ribbon Bows Gift Box By Gail Pierce-Watne

how to: Wrap box in silk fabric. Cut a piece of crinkled paper to fit around box, trim ends with decorative scissors, wrap around box and adhere. To create each bow, cut two pieces of ribbon measuring 9 inches and 2 inches. Fold the longer length to create two loops and tack in the middle to hold in place. Wrap the smaller ribbon around the middle and adhere on the back. Place three bows down the middle of the wrapped box.

ribbon
ACCENTS

the final touch

Vintage Tag Set By Jayme Shepherd

how to: Cut cardstock into tag shapes and add paper or other embellishments. Wrap and tie various types and textures of ribbon around tags to decorate. Create tabs by folding and stapling strips of ribbon to top, attaching with brad or piece of decorative trim or tying through the hole. Decorate a small tin box with paper, ribbon and trim and place tag set inside.

RIBBON

flowers

sewing

tying

wrapping

attaching

looping

accents

tassels

For hundreds of years, ribbon has been used to beautify the home. Not only for its decorative quality but for its practical

utility as well. From trimming the earliest tapestries to hanging modern wall décor, there's a ribbon for every style, need

and decorating whim. Take a look around your rooms to see where you could add a little pizzazz. Then use the ideas here

to make ribbon a welcome and easy addition to your home.

home décor

ribbon flowers
simple

Lotus Flower Candle Votive
By Hosanna Houser

how to: Create three folded ribbon leaves with a wide satin ribbon. Cut a long length of sheer ribbon and twist and loop working in a circular pattern until flower petals are formed. Staple ribbon together in the center. Place leaves under flower and staple in place. Position glass votive in the middle of flower and add candle to hide staples.

moderate

intricate

how to: Create a lotus flower. Double a second length of sheer ribbon with a length of flower trim. Twist and loop to create another layer of petals. Staple onto top of flower and add candle and votive.

how to: Create a lotus flower. Cut a long length of sheer ribbon in a complementary color and loop until large flower is formed. Secure loops with several stitches in the center and stitch top flower to lotus flower.

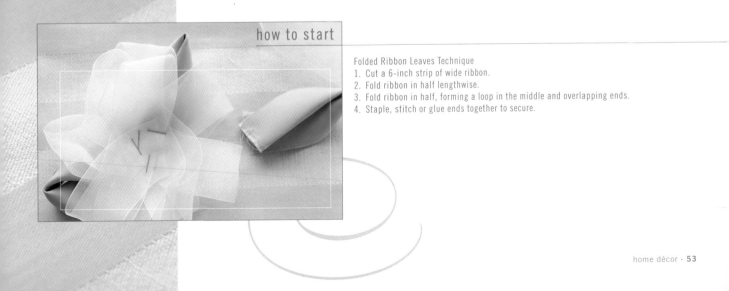

how to start

Folded Ribbon Leaves Technique
1. Cut a 6-inch strip of wide ribbon.
2. Fold ribbon in half lengthwise.
3. Fold ribbon in half, forming a loop in the middle and overlapping ends.
4. Staple, stitch or glue ends together to secure.

sewing RIBBON

Baby Garland
By Jennifer Jensen

how to: Cut 36-inch piece of wide ribbon for garland base. Cut approximately 65 strips of 3½ to 4½-inch ribbon and fabric (may require more or less depending on widths). Lay base on a flat surface and, starting 4 inches in from one end, lay one strip across top of base and one piece under base. Continue alternating strips along base to 4 inches in from other end. Strips should slightly overlap so that there are no spaces in between. Pin strips in place and machine stitch down center of base to attach. Hang embellished photos and other accents from clips and tie clips to garland with ribbon.

Hanging Monogram

By Lynne Montgomery

how to: Cover wood monogram with Word Fetti and trim edges with razor blade. Paint edges of letter and dry brush around edges of front, overlapping stickers. Coat piece with decoupage medium and let dry. String Ribbon Charm Alphabet letters and tie strips of ribbon onto metal hoop earring. Drill hole into top of letter, thread ribbon through, tie embellished earring to ribbon, tie ribbon closed and hang.

tying RIBBON

JOURNEY (jur´-ne)

essence of someth
necessities; indis

DESTINATION (des´
place of which

hazardous underta
exciting, often s

EXPE
of l

TRAV
othe
2. st
tim

Dis

to be the fir

wrapping WITH RIBBON

Candle Set
By Kris Stanger

how to: Adhere Defined Clear stickers to
candles. Wrap a variety of ribbons around
candles in graduating heights, securing with
Ribbon Attachments or knots.

attaching with RIBBON

TREASURE EACH DAY

Ribbon Frame
By Mellette Berezoski

how to: Remove backing and glass from frame and distress edges with paint. Tie ribbon around one side of frame, wrap around in a zigzag pattern and tie to opposite side to secure. Place silk flower in opening, intertwining with ribbon and tie ribbon around stem. Add photo and embellishments and attach corner brackets to the back of the frame so that it is self-standing.

knotting RIBBON

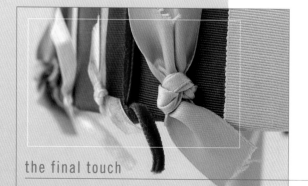

the final touch

Flower Lamp
By Jennifer Jensen

how to: Cover lampshade with fabric. Wrap a variety of ribbons vertically around shade, knotting at the bottom. Make sure ribbon is pulled tight. Paint Eyelet Charms, add center and adhere.

tying

Flower Pillow
By Jennifer Jensen

how to: Measure size of pillow and cut rectangle from fabric that is twice as long as pillow. Fold in half, right sides together, and machine stitch three sides together. Turn right side out and fold down unstitched edge twice. Press and stitch to create cuff. Cut eight pairs of 12-inch strips of ribbon, pin along inside of cuff across from each other and stitch to attach. Slide cover onto pillow and tie ribbon pairs together. Paint Eyelet Charms, add centers and stitch or glue onto pillow along seam.

another look

RIBBON *flowers*

Shadow Box
By Loni Stevens

how to: Cut foam core to fit frame and cut out four openings of equal sizes. Line inside of cuts with ribbon, attaching with small pins. Back foam core with Metal Mesh and dark cardstock. Fill in three squares with flowers made by layering looped and gathered ribbons. Use mini brads and vintage button for centers. Attach monogram in fourth opening.

*ribbon*CLOSURES

Pillow Shams

By Jayme Shepherd

how to: Slide pillow form into first of two pillowcases and set aside. With second pillowcase, fold opening to the inside just above the seam and press. Using a needle and thread, stitch four pairs of ribbon to sides of opening. Insert pillow into second pillowcase and tie ribbons together to close.

Monogram
By Margie Romney-Aslett

how to: Stamp letter with paint and, when dry, tie several strips of ribbon around letter where desired. Thread embellishments onto a Trinket Pin and pass through one of the knots.

tying RIBBON

looping RIBBON

Topiary
By Maggie Holmes

how to: Cut 4½-inch strips from a variety of coordinating ribbons and trims. For best results, use several widths, patterns and textures. Create ribbon loops and attach to foam ball until completely covered. Paint dowel and insert into bottom of ball. Cut florist foam to fit inside tin pot and insert other end of dowel into foam. Cover with moss and wrap ribbon around pot.

how to start

LOOPING RIBBON TECHNIQUE
1. Form circle with strip of ribbon, overlapping ends.
2. Slide ends over each other to adjust size of circle.
3. Holding ends together with fingers, insert pin or other attachment through both layers.
4. Attach loop to desired surface.

ribbon ACCENTS

change it up

Tri-Fold Frame

By Charla Campbell

how to: Wrap lace vertically around edge of one frame. Cover most of front of a second frame with a fabric swatch and trim to fit. Punch holes along edge of photo to go on third frame and tie ribbon strips through. Attach photos to frames, add additional embellishments and attach together with hinges to create tri-fold frame.

Try stacking the photos and displaying them in a box or basket instead of creating the frame. Layer petals cut from silk ribbon to decorate the container.

RIBBON *tassels*

Table Runner

By Mellette Berezoski

how to: Cut two pieces of fabric to desired length and width. Machine sew along edges with right sides together leaving a 5-inch opening on one edge. Press and trim seams and pull through opening to turn right side out. Press edge and hand stitch opening to close. Top stitch two rows around edges. Create tassels with several different coordinating ribbons and stitch to ends. Add vintage buttons.

RIBBON

weaving

printing

making

hinges　　*accents*

tying

distressing

borders

pleating　　*flowers*

embroidery

fringe　*layering*

gathering

Richly symbolic, ribbon has long been used to recognize military achievement, decorate battle flags, welcome home a loved one, bring awareness to a social issue or make a political statement. Use it to give meaning and symbolism to your scrapbooks, to reinforce a theme or simply as an attractive accent. With the ideas in this chapter you can add a little or a lot of ribbon to your pages to create layouts that you'll love.

scrapbook pages

ribbon weaving
intricate

CHERUB (cher´əb) 1. a type of angel characterized as a chubby, rosy cheeked child with wings 2. a child with a sweet, innocent face

Happy Baby By Loni Stevens

how to: Use a pencil and ruler to lightly trace a grid onto background, making the spaces the same width as the ribbon to be used. With a craft knife, cut slits at the top of every other square, flip paper over and weave ribbon strips through using tweezers to pull them through slits. Once all vertical lines have been woven, weave ribbon horizontally until entire background is filled. Trim ends and stitch a frame around edge to secure.

moderate

simple

how to: Trim cardstock to create the size of flap that will fit the page. Use the same weaving technique on the flap, trimming ends and stitching a frame around edges to secure. Attach to page using hinges and add embellishments, photos or journaling underneath.

how to: Use weaving technique around outside edge of cardstock to create a border that is one ribbon-width thick. Secure ends on the back using adhesive and mount to a larger piece of cardstock. Attach photos to cardstock block and adhere to page slightly overlapping edges of border.

the final touch

PRINTING ON *ribbon*

Madison 2004

By Lynne Montgomery

how to: Cut twisted muslin into four equal
blocks. Spray adhere onto background
cardstock, alternating so that the top left
and bottom right blocks lay horizontally
and the top right and bottom left blocks
lay vertically. Cross stitch with linen thread
along edges and seams to secure pieces.
Attach printed ribbon strips with mini brads
and staples.

PRINTING ON RIBBON TECHNIQUE
1. Print desired text onto paper.
2. Use spray adhesive to temporarily attach
   ribbon directly over text.
3. Run paper through printer again, this time
   transferring text to ribbon.

how to start

bliss (blis) 1. great happ.... 2. spirit...

GLOW
1. TO GIVE OFF
BRIGHT LIGHT
2. to be elate
3. a countenance
reflects great joy

distressing **RIBBON**

SheLBY

Shelby By Kris Stanger

how to: Cut and fray edges of a piece of fabric that is slightly smaller than background. Soak fabric and piece of silk ribbon in a boiling tea bath for several minutes, lay onto a cookie sheet and bake for roughly 15 minutes, watching carefully at all times. When dry, attach to background and secure corners with Decorative Brads. Tie silk ribbon through Ribbon Charm and position just below photo.

ribbon **HINGES**

ANNOUNCED BY ALL THE TRUMPETS OF THE SKY, ARRIVES THE SNOW.

Ralph Waldo Emerson

LIFT HERE

magic [winter wonderland]

Winter Wonderland

By Loni Stevens

how to: Cut four 2-inch strips of Woven Ribbon. Fold one side of each strip under and stitch, leaving an opening to thread elastic through and stitch along the opposite edges. Run elastic through openings, pull tightly and secure. Space evenly and adhere to photo, paper or embellishment to create ribbon hinges.

how to start

CUSTOM STRIPES TECHNIQUE
1. Cut wide striped ribbon to desired length.
2. Cut thin ribbon to same length and adhere over stripe or stripes to cover.
3. Resulting ribbon will be a custom color scheme.

ribbon **ACCENTS**

SoliTudE **ESCAPE:**
1. a getaway
2. leave stress and worries behind
3. REFRESH AND RELAX
4. mental release FROM REALITY

time alone

the final touch

Solitude

By Erin Terrell

how to: Mix aging ink and place in container with a spray nozzle. Spray ribbon with dye and let dry. Attach strips to top of photo with staples. Thread another strip through staples and knot. Slide Ribbon Charm Alphabet letters onto ribbon for title and attach along bottom.

tying **RIBBON AND FABRIC**

Remember When...

By Lynne Montgomery

how to: Attach muslin to background cardstock with spray adhesive. Scan old book paper and print onto muslin. Fray edges of a painted piece of fabric and attach to layout. Wrap printed twill tape and trim around top and bottom edges and tie strips of ribbon and fabric down left side of layout.

the final touch

antiquing **RIBBON**

Bébé

By Kris Stanger

how to: Paint Jigsaw Alphabet letters, let dry and lightly rub pigment ink over edges to antique. Rub pigment ink over printed ribbon, wrap around first letter in title and stitch to secure. Attach letters across bottom and add vintage flowers along fabric border.

Family By Kris Stanger

how to: Tie ends of two strips of ribbon to a ribbon clasp and trim. Attach clasp in bottom right corner of photo and lay ribbon strips flat along edges of photo. Cut slits in the top and left edges of background, pass ribbons through and trim ends so that they overhang slightly.

the final touch

tying RIBBON

Giggle By Maggie Holmes

how to: Cut a series of vertical slits across a rectangle of paper approximately 1 inch down from top edge. Thread a variety of ribbon strips through and knot. Attach across bottom of layout. Create a photo frame by overlapping four strips of ribbon and stitching.

happy

walking with Dad
American Girl dolls
my soft blanket
cuddling up by Mom
getting my allowance
my birthday
macaroni and cheese
visiting art museums
my big brothers
learning Spanish
airplane rides
softball and swimming
painting a picture
everything Christmas
reading books
finding a penny

Jillian 2005

pleating RIBBON

Happy By Julie Turner

how to: Adhere a strip of Woven Ribbon vertically down page to separate photo and journaling. Pleat a length of ribbon, stitching down the middle and adhere in a wavy line across bottom half of page.

ribbon
WEAVING

the final touch

NAME Emily

FOLIO 7

BOX NUMBERS 1 2 3 4 5 6 7

thanks

...for always telling the truth and having the courage to tell me when you have made a mistake.

...for being brave and trying new activities like soccer, dance, and softball.

...for being self motivated when it comes to reading. I can barely get a book out of your hands.

...for trying hard in school and getting good grades.

...for letting me style your hair the way I like even though it may not be your favorite.

...for always being a willing and happy participant when it is time for another photo shoot.

...for supporting your father and I when it comes to attending church, holding family prayer, family scripture study, and family home evenings.

...for being a peacemaker. I appreciate you sharing and playing with your brother and sister even though it may not be easy.

...for being silly and making me smile.

...for your hugs and kisses.

Thanks for being you!

December 2004

Thanks By Lynne Montgomery

how to: Stipple ribbon with walnut ink to give it an aged appearance. Cut a series of slits through a wide ribbon and weave a thinner ribbon or trim through for a layered look. String Ribbon Charm Alphabet letters onto ribbon and tie at ends to hold letters in place.

RIBBON *embroidery*

Do your **part** to make this **world** a **cuter** place to **live** in.

— SUSAN BRANCH

FEB. 2005

GIRLY [GIRL]

Girly Girl
By Mellette Berezoski

how to: Lightly pencil flower designs on layout and poke holes to mark stitches. Backstitch with ribbon to create stems. Create flower petals by stitching ribbon with a lazy daisy stitch. Tie ribbon in French knots for leaves and add a button and snap as centers.

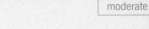

RIBBON *flowers*

MO•M ENT•S

(a collection of moments.)

fun (fun) 1. lively, joyous play or playfulness pleasure 2. a source of amusement

precious

how to start

RIBBON FLOWERS TECHNIQUE

1. Punch a 3/16-inch hole on background.
2. Punch five 1/8-inch holes in a circle around 3/16-inch hole.
3. From the back, bring a ribbon up through the large center hole and pass it down through one of the small holes. Tack down the end on the back so that ribbon doesn't pull all the way through.
4. Bring ribbon back up through center hole and pass down through next small hole.
5. Repeat, working in a circular pattern, until a flower is created. When finished, trim ribbon and adhere end on the back.

Moments

By Loni Stevens

how to: Stitch diagonal lines across background ½-inch apart. Create several flowers randomly spaced on stitched background using Ribbon Flowers technique. Use a variety of coordinating ribbons for interest.

RIBBON *fringe*

the final touch

Adore You By Jennifer Jensen

how to: Fold several 2-inch strips of ribbon and lightly tack to the back of bottom left corner of photo. Place on layout and zigzag stitch to attach. Twist a 10-inch piece of ribbon to create a loop, place in bottom right corner of photo and stitch ends along edges of photo. Add Gameboard Shape flower where ribbon crosses to embellish. Stitch trim or ribbon to cover paper seams.

knotting
RIBBON

PLAY MATES
SIDEKICK
HOOLIGANS

As a parent, I realize it's my responsibility to watch out for Daisy's best interests and to discipline her to the best of my abilities.

However, it sure is fun to just set aside the parenting role every now and then and just be friends with my little girl! We have the most fun when we play and act like sisters!

One of our favorite things to do is play beauty shop. We'll style each other's hair and put makeup on each other, then pose for silly pictures to show off the end result!

girlfriends
COMRADES

Sidekick

By Erin Terrell

how to: Attach ribbon across page as desired. Punch a series of holes through the center of ribbon and pull contrasting strips of ribbon through. Knot strips on front, trim ends and tack down ends on back.

layering RIBBON

Girlfriends By Jennifer Jensen

how to: Overlap pieces of wide ribbon in a variety of textures across layout. Straight stitch down center to attach.
Add title and rub-ons on top of ribbon.

layering ribbon **AND FABRIC**

My Daughter By Kris Stanger

how to: Create flower accent by layering silk flower and flower shapes cut from various fabrics and tulle. Place in bottom right corner of frame opening and staple through to secure. Place button and hatpin in the middle to create the center.

the final touch

Shades of Chloe By Jennifer Jensen

how to: Create background using Fabric Strip Background technique. Turn over and trace inside letters from Jigsaw Alphabet in reverse. Using a craft knife or small, sharp scissors, cut around traced lines. Cut a piece of cardstock for backing, paint desired color and attach pieces together. Paint remaining letters from title with same paint and attach on top of fabric. Print text and photo onto fabric, arrange on layout and attach.

FABRIC STRIP BACKGROUND TECHNIQUE
1. Cut background cardstock to size.
2. Assemble several coordinating fabrics. Snip edge of fabric and tear down length into ½-inch to 1-inch strips.
3. Starting at bottom of page, start laying strips horizontally across cardstock and lightly tack into place with adhesive.
4. Continue up the page until completely covered.
5. Start machine stitching vertically ½ inch in from edge of page. Continue stitching lines across the page at ½-inch intervals.

how to start

gathering RIBBON

Springtime
By Julie Turner

how to: Cut cardstock in the same color as background into four equal strips. Punch large holes down strips, back some with colored cardstock or journaling and attach to background. Cut flowers from trim and add to centers of colored circles. Tightly gather a strip of thin ribbon and stretch it vertically along page. Wrap around edge and adhere on back. Tie ribbon next to gathered ribbon and dangle an Eyelet Letter from a jump ring.

party ideas

RIBBON

lacing

stitching

embellishments

wrapping

accents

knotting

gathering

In Victorian England, traditional weddings included a ribbon pull. Before the bride and groom cut the cake, the bridesmaids would gather around the table and pull a ribbon out of the cake to reveal a sterling silver charm—and her future. There are many other ways to invite ribbon to your gatherings and occasions. In this chapter, you'll find inventive ideas for featuring it at your next get-together so that it becomes the life of the party.

party ideas

lacing ribbon
intricate

Baby Shower By Joanna Bolick

how to: Frame a quote, wrap ribbon around bottom right corner of frame and embellish with Charmed. Using two lengths of coordinating ribbon, lace baby shoes, adding Ribbon Letter Wraps to spell desired words.

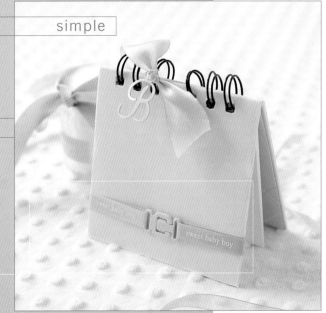

how to: Wrap Ribbon Words around the front cover of a mini spiral notebook and attach with a ribbon clasp. Tie Eyelet Letter to one of the spirals with a wide ribbon.

how to: Paint blocks, stamp and wrap ribbon around edges. Print invitation onto cardstock, mat, punch holes in the top and thread ribbon through to complete.

change it up

Change the color of shoes and ribbon to match the gender of the baby. And string other charms or accents onto ribbon to embellish.

stitching with **RIBBON**

Girls' Day Out
By Robyn Werlich

how to: Gather strip of ribbon and adhere over cardstock on front of invitations to embellish. With a large sewing needle, stitch ribbon flowers to tops of slippers and add French knots in the centers. Stitch similar flowers onto hand towel cut to cover a small pillow form. Stitch cover closed, wrap end over and knot ribbons down the side to close.

ribbon ACCENTS

Spring Brunch
By Kris Stanger

how to: Tie ribbon around top of ceramic watering can. Layer patterned cardstock and ribbon to create embellished napkin rings. Fold small strips of ribbon, place under Blossoms to make leaves and attach to placemat. Fold decorative edged cardstock in half to create a 3½ x 4½-inch card. Wrap patterned cardstock, ribbon and rickrack around top flap to embellish, print party information on vellum and secure inside with mini brads.

the final touch

wrapping WITH RIBBON

Birthday Party
By Maggie Holmes

how to: For invitation, attach ribbon vertically to cardstock square with brads and staples and slide printed information underneath. Tie strips of ribbon around stem of glass. Wrap ribbon around glass votive holder, fold back end and secure with a brad. Wrap strips of ribbon around larger glass jar, secure with Ribbon Attachments and fill with candy. For the placemat, stitch a piece of 6x12-inch paper to the edge of a 12x12-inch piece of League paper. Cut a rectangle of tulle, add ribbon tabs and Blossom to front with brads and stitch to side of mat to create a pocket. Slide utensils through tabs and napkin in pocket.

RIBBON *embellishments*

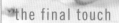

the final touch

Bridal Shower
By Hosanna Houser

how to: Create wrapped "gifts" on the front of plain cards using a combination of wide and narrow ribbons for invitations. To make table runner, cut nine lengths of wide ribbon in coordinating colors. Stitch long edges together starting and ending 8 inches in from ends. Knot ends and trim excess if necessary. Wrap three wide ribbons around a square vase, placing all seams down the middle of one side. Fold a 9-inch section of ribbon to create two loops, wrap a 2-inch section around middle and adhere to create a bow. Attach vertically onto vase, covering seams. Wrap ribbon around soap to use as a favor and place card.

RIBBON *embellishments*

Princess and the Pea Party

By Jennifer Jensen

how to: Tie organza ribbon around straps of flip-flops until covered. Cut flowers from trim, adhere to ends of ribbon and add rhinestones as centers. Measure elastic to fit around waist, cut and stitch ends together. Tie long lengths of ribbon to elastic until it is covered to create a skirt or tutu. Cut flowers from trim, adhere to random ends of ribbon and add rhinestones as centers.

the final touch

how to: Stitch two rectangles and a thin layer of batting together to make a pillow. Repeat to create a second pillow. Stack and tie together with ribbon. Print invitation onto cardstock and slide under ribbon. Cut peapod shape from felt, add buttons and attach to ribbon. Thread beads and tied ribbon strips onto elastic cording. Wrap bracelet around a pair of gloves, label with name of guest and use as place card and favor. To create a goodie bag, weave ribbon in and out of the edges of a crocheted doily. Fill with trinkets, gather and tie ribbons together and tie another ribbon around the top to close.

intricate

gifts

RIBBON

detailing

backgrounds

attachments

accents *sewing*

gifts

One of the first encounters we have with ribbons is a beautifully wrapped birthday gift. And that festive association continues throughout our lives. Ribbons are used to adorn and decorate holidays and to mark and celebrate milestones. But more than just topping a gift, ribbon can be the gift. The projects in this chapter incorporate ribbon to create meaningful keepsakes your recipients will treasure now and for years to come.

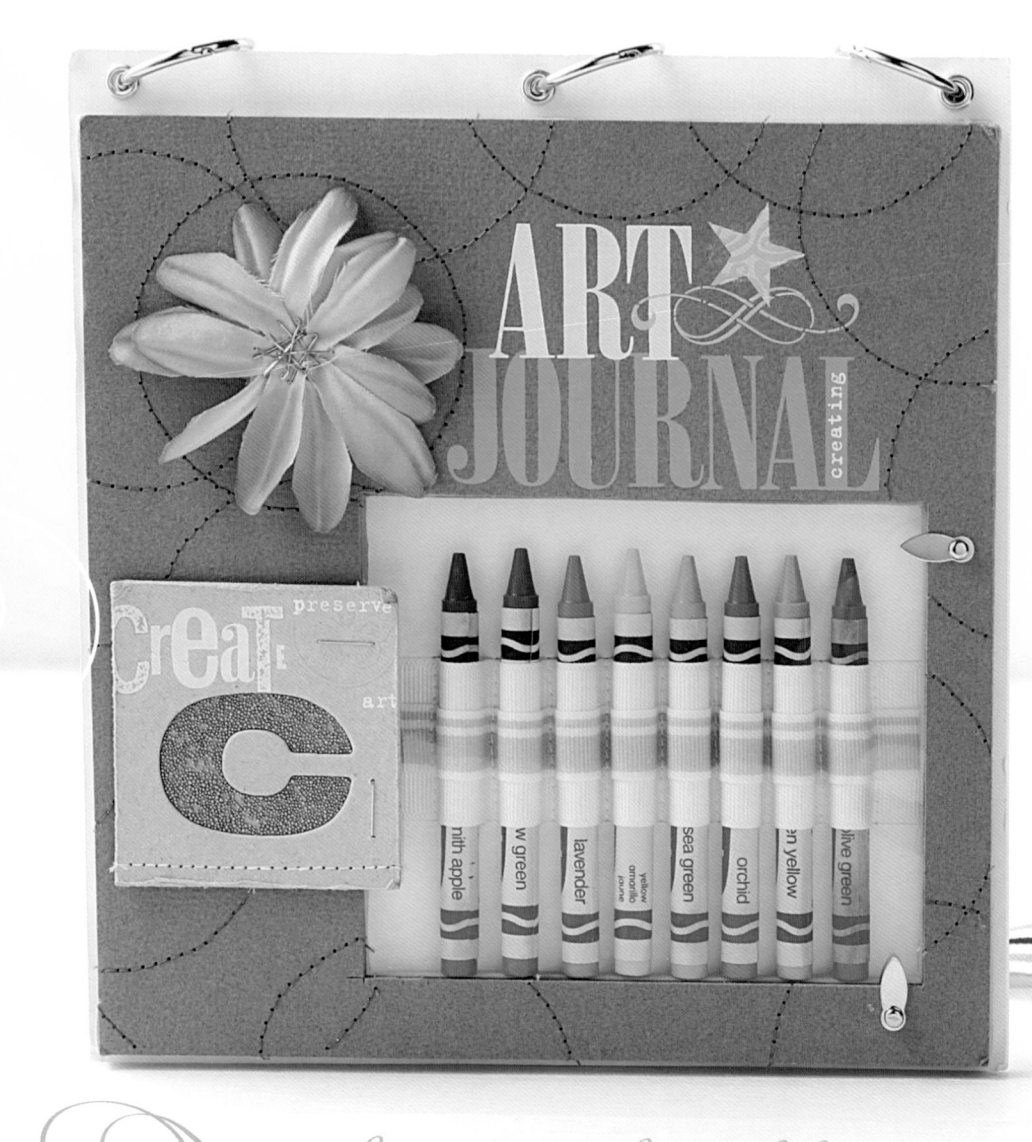

Art Journal
By Loni Stevens

how to: Draw a pencil line across white cardstock to use as a guide. Cut two ribbons 4 to 5 inches longer than length of crayon holder, layer and adhere together. Starting on left side, wrap ribbon around left edge of cardstock and stitch vertically along ribbon where crayons will start. Place crayon on cardstock, wrap ribbon over it and adhere with a thin strip of double-sided tape. Stitch over tape and repeat process across cardstock until desired numbers of holders is created. Cut foam core to fit front cover of journal, cut opening out of bottom right corner and adhere card-stock with crayons behind. Embellish rest of foam core and attach to cover.

detailing with ribbon
intricate

how to: Trim paper to wrap around front and back covers of Mini Book, layer and attach. Adhere MM Kids Trim across the back of the book, wrap ends around to the front and tie pen to book. Apply rub-ons for title.

how to: **Measure around book, add an extra 5 inches for closure and** holders and cut ribbon. Leaving backing on, mark Fabric Tape where pencil holders will be and adhere ribbon, stitching pencil holders in place. Carefully remove backing and adhere to book, wrapping around to back. Trim excess Fabric Tape but not ribbon. Bring excess ribbon around to front, fold under and adhere to create a tab. Wrap a strip of ribbon around tab vertically and stitch. Attach both sides of a snap under ribbon tab to create closure. Clip prongs from Decorative Brad and adhere.

the final touch

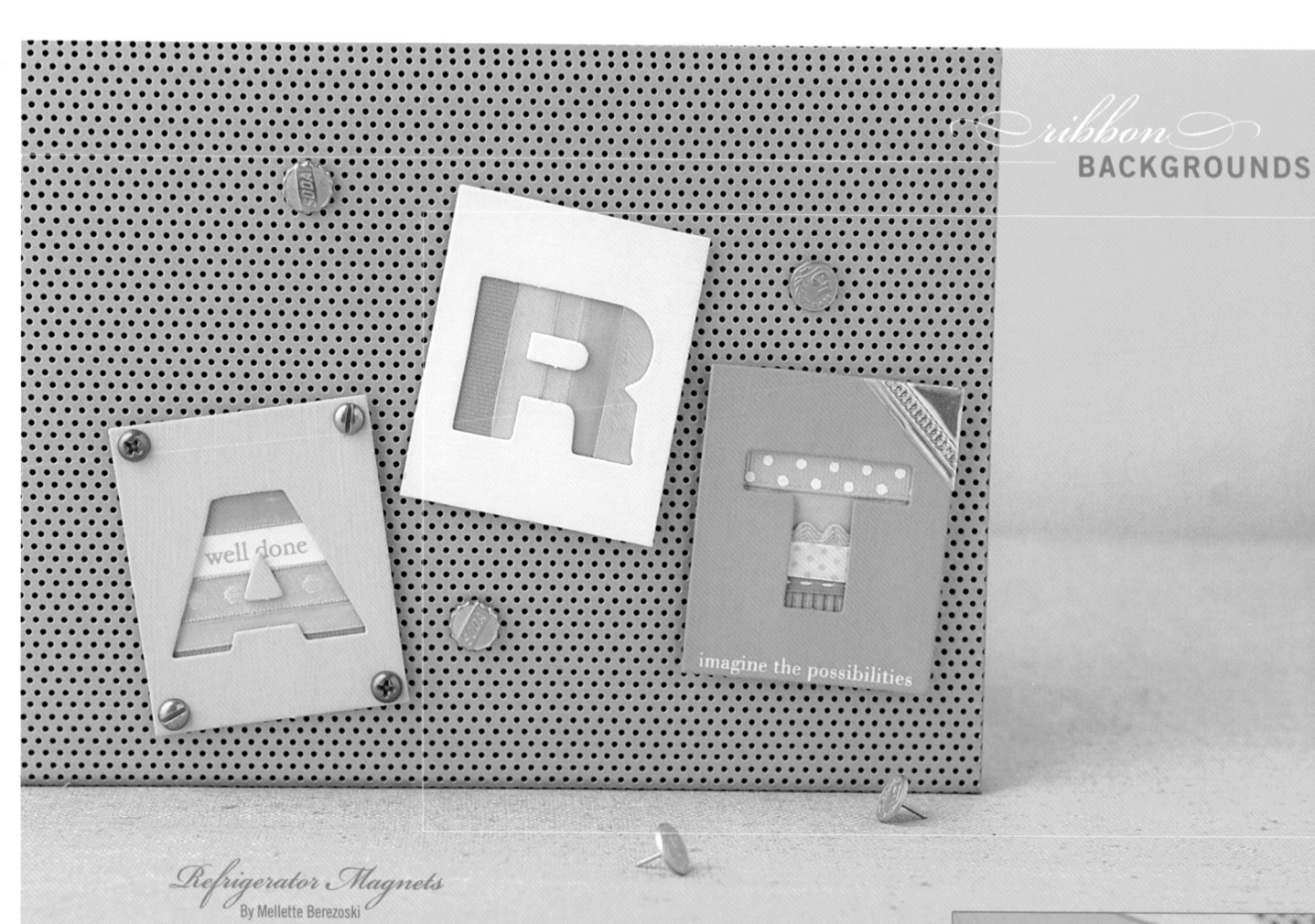

Refrigerator Magnets
By Mellette Berezoski

how to: Paint negative sections of Jigsaw Alphabet letters in coordinating colors. Fill in letters using Layered Background technique. Add embellishments to front of letters and magnet strips to back.

how to start

LAYERED BACKGROUND TECHNIQUE
1. Cut cardstock backing to same size as Jigsaw Alphabet letter.
2. Trace letter through stencil onto backing.
3. Layer of ribbon and trim on backing until traced letter is covered.
4. Attach stencil to backing and add embellishments.

ribbon ATTACHMENTS

Bookmarks
By Erin Terrell

how to: Weave one end of long length of ribbon through a Ribbon Charm and pull excess back under. Secure ribbon together with a mini brad.

embellishing with **RIBBON**

First Aid Kit

By Loni Stevens

how to: Fold oven mitt in half and hand stitch button onto side opposite loop. Loop and button will create closure when kit is finished. Stitch and iron on ribbon and trim and add further embellishments to outside. Inside, stitch snack bags along center and fill with first aid items.

another look

ribbon
ACCENTS

Baby Gear
By Janet Hopkins

how to: Stitch rickrack around bottom of washcloths leaving a small unstitched space in the middle. Loop ribbon through unstitched section, tie and dangle a charm from a jump ring. Tie ribbons around tops of bottles and dangle painted Charmed Plaques Mini from bows using jump rings. Loop one end of a long length of ribbon through pacifier and stitch to close. Loop the other end, stitch to close and use for attaching. Place items in a basket spray painted to match.

ribbon
BACKGROUNDS

Glass Paper Weight
By Lynne Montgomery

how to: Adhere old book paper to cardstock
and attach ribbon strips on top. Measure diameter
of bottom of paper weight, turn cardstock
piece over and use a circle cutter to cut it to fit.
Attach embellishments over ribbon and adhere
circle to bottom of paper weight.

Watch and Box Gift Set

By Kris Stanger

how to: Cut two strips of ribbon to create watch band. Loop one end and through watch face and the other end through rectangle ring and secure with studs. Trim excess ribbon. Wire toggle clasp to rectangle ring ends. Paint box, let dry and ink. Glue ribbon around edge of lid, add ribbon and Leather Flower to tag and add message.

attaching with **RIBBON**

moderate

fashion & jewelry

sewing

gathering

embellishments

attaching

weaving

knotting

During the 17th and 18th centuries, French fashion was dictated by one simple rule—you can never have enough ribbon. It lavishly embellished nearly every inch of clothing from delicate rosettes to intricate embroidery. One men's garment from the period is trimmed with 250 yards of ribbon! While you may not use quite that much, you can still add style and flair to your own fashions with the projects you'll find in this chapter.

fashion & jewelry

sewing ribbon
intricate

Girl's Jeans
By Jennifer Jensen

how to: Stitch a long sewing machine stitch along the length of wide grosgrain ribbon and pull ends to gather. Pin gathered and other coordinating ribbon along the bottom hems of jeans, layering some ribbon and trim if desired and stitch to attach. Stitch strips of rickrack along tops of cargo pockets. Cut flowers from trim and stitch above hem and to ends of drawstrings.

moderate

simple

how to: Cut ribbon into 1-inch pieces. Fold to create tabs and pin to inside of pockets, fly and under Woven Label. Using a needle and thread, stitch tabs to jeans and label to secure and stitch label to back pocket.

how to: Stitch lengths of ribbon to dress following hemline. Create a bow, attach to neckline and embellish with flower trim.

the final touch

*sewing*RIBBON

Ribbon Watch

By Margie Romney-Aslett

how to: Center a strip of ribbon on top of a wider one, pin in place and stitch to attach together. Fold one end around two d-rings and stitch. Thread through pins on watch face and trim end in a v-cut at proper length. Create several color variations to change band as desired.

RIBBON *embellishments*

Birthday Tag
By Kim McCrary

how to: Cut a 5½-inch strip of wide ribbon, fold edges in on one end and adhere to create a point. Fold pointed end over 1 inch, fold up the long end and tuck under point. Secure point to folded ribbon underneath with a mini brad. Bend wire to create the shape of a letter "D". String beads onto curved part of wire, slide straight part onto ribbon purse and bend ends together to close. Apply rub-ons to tag, attach purse and tag together with bead chain and hang from purse handle.

attaching with RIBBON

Handbag Ribbon Belts
By Mellette Berezoski

how to: Cut ribbons to double the desired length. Fold in half and position lanyard clasps on fold. Tie one ribbon in a knot approximately 1½ inches above clasp and attach Eyelet Tag Alphabet to knot with jump rings. On the other ribbon, thread Ribbon Charm Alphabet letters and attach studs to keep them in place. Stitch ends with right sides together to finish.

another look

RIBBON

Woven Watch

By Loni Stevens

how to: Attach chains to both sides of watch face using jump rings. Weave ribbon through links, folding under and stitching ends. Tie a big bow with an extra length of ribbon on one end.

sewing RIBBON

the final touch

Cosmetic Bag
By Maggie Holmes

how to: Remove handles from a store-bought cosmetic bag. Create ribbon handles by threading a wide ribbon through metal rings, folding ends under and stitching to attach. Adhere ribbon to sides and bottom of bag, threading through bottoms of metal rings, folding ends under and stitching to secure. Create flower using fabric and tulle and attach to bag to embellish.

knotting
RIBBON

Flower Choker
By Erin Terrell

how to: Measure neck, add an extra 10 to 12 inches and cut ribbon. Slide a Leather Flower onto ribbon, tie a loose knot and thread end of ribbon back down through center. Knot will hold flower in place. Repeat until desired number of flowers are on ribbon and tie around neck.

children & teen projects

tying

backgrounds

borders

layering

accents

attaching

knotting

One of the most widely known ribbon traditions is the dance around the maypole. A traditional rite of spring, ribbons are intertwined in distinct weaves as young women perform ceremonial and highly choreographed dances around the pole. If the maypole isn't quite the ribboncraft for your kids, let them peruse the following pages. They just might find something they like in the projects we've designed just for them.

children & teen projects

tying ribbon
intricate

Flip-Flops

By Jennifer and Addison Jensen

how to: Cut ribbon and trim of various widths and textures into strips measuring 4½ or 5 inches in length. Tie strips in tight double knots around plastic straps, making sure that strips are close together with no visible space in between. Where straps meet, add a Ribbon Charm Alphabet letter to one of the strips before tying.

simple

moderate

how to: **Trim** ribbon to cover plastic straps on flip-flop. Place double-sided tape on straps and adhere ribbon. Create a folded flower with same ribbon. Stitch button to the center of the flower and stitch the flower to the top of the flip-flop.

how to: **Adhere** ribbon to straps of flip-flop with double-sided tape. Thread two beads onto a strand of beading floss and tie floss to a length of ribbon. Trim ends of floss if necessary. Tie beaded ribbons to strap of flip-flop with a knot so that beads are positioned on top.

how to start

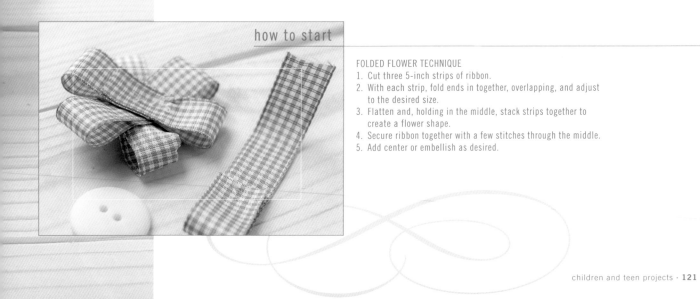

FOLDED FLOWER TECHNIQUE
1. Cut three 5-inch strips of ribbon.
2. With each strip, fold ends in together, overlapping, and adjust to the desired size.
3. Flatten and, holding in the middle, stack strips together to create a flower shape.
4. Secure ribbon together with a few stitches through the middle.
5. Add center or embellish as desired.

ribbon
BACKGROUNDS

Memo Board By Mellette Berezoski and Maysie Ocera

how to: Attach several coordinating ribbons vertically along left side of board wrapping ends around edges. Secure to the back with a staple gun. Weave ribbon horizontally through vertical ribbons and secure ends to back with staple gun. Add Ribbon Attachments to any ribbon before stapling, if desired.

CRIBBON *borders*

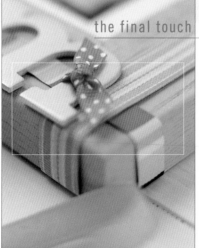

the final touch

Bordered Frame

By Margie and Megan Aslett

how to: Paint frame desired color. Wrap ribbon around each edge, securing ends on the back of the frame or knotting on the front. Add rhinestone buckle to top left corner. Tie strip of ribbon around Monogram and place in bottom right corner.

lipgloss

change it up

nailpolish

Try throwing in a few touches of a complementary color to a mostly monochromatic color scheme. Here, green is perfectly paired with purple.

Ribbon-Wrapped Container

By Mellette Berezoski and Maysie Ocera

how to: Starting at the top, wrap and glue a variety of coordinating ribbons around each container, overlapping to completely cover box. Add metal embellishments and letters as desired. Line ends up on the back and, when container is covered, glue a strip of ribbon over seam to cover.

tying RIBBON

Team Photo Book

By Kris and Kennedy Stanger

how to: Cover a photo or memorabilia album with patterned cardstock. Tie various strips of ribbon to spiral binding and add additional embellishments.

Double Frame By Julie and Jackson Turner

how to: Remove all backing from two matching frames and glue glass into opening. Use Ribbon Edging technique to create border around frame opening. Glue or attach embellishments, photos and Metal Mesh to glass and frames. Screw three eyelet screws into the sides of each frame and tie together with ribbon so that frames stand up.

RIBBON EDGING TECHNIQUE

1. Once all backing is removed from a picture frame, turn it over.
2. Adhere strips of ribbon (a patterned ribbon works best) along edge of opening.
3. Add photo and backing and turn over. Edges of ribbon will be visible from the front.

how to start

Ribbon borders

wrapping WITH RIBBON

Art Project Holder

By Jayme and Brayden Shepherd

how to: Cut wood to desired length, paint and lightly sand. Trim photos to size and decoupage along top edge to attach. Adhere strips of ribbon along bottom edge of photos, wrapping around and securing on the back. Add other embellishments and attach small magnetic clips.

NOTES

ribbon **ACCENTS**

Message Center Clip

By Janet and Taylor Hopkins

how to: Apply rub-ons to clip. Tie strips of coordinating ribbon to bottom of the clip, knotting on the front. Add printed Cardstock Tag to one of the strips.

from

mOm

the final touch

Lip Gloss Lanyard
By Margie and Brooke Aslett

how to: Fold a long strand of Woven Ribbon in half. With ends together, wrap around a key ring and secure all layers of ribbon with two Crystal Brads. Paint Eyelet Letter, string with Eyelet Shape onto safety pin and fasten to jump ring on lip gloss. Clip lip gloss to key ring.

attaching with
RIBBON

knotting
RIBBON

Bracelet

By Julie and Jillian Turner

how to: Cut long length of sheer ribbon. String pearls onto ribbon knotting in between each one. Add one pearl on both ends of ribbon, securing in place with a knot on either side. Tie to wrist with a big bow.

layering ribbon AND FABRIC

Headbands By Erin and Daisy Terrell

how to: Cover large headband with Fabric Tape and use double-sided tape to adhere ribbon along center. Fold and layer various strips of ribbon in graduating sizes and attach to top. Coat small headband with spray adhesive and wrap ribbon around until covered. Add embellished flower to top of both pieces.

another look

supply lists

CHAPTER 2

Flower Card (intricate)
Crystal brad, matchbook card base
and insert, MM kids trim and scrapbook
colors acrylic paint: Making Memories
Other: Fabric and tulle

Flower Card (moderate)
Matchbook card base and insert, MM
kids trim, petals and scrapbook colors
acrylic paint: Making Memories

Flower Card (simple)
Blossoms, matchbook card base and
insert, mini brad and MM kids trim:
Making Memories

Our Sincere Thanks
Vintage hip trim and window card
base and insert: Making Memories
Stamp: Hero Arts
Stamping ink: Ranger Industries
Other: Transparency

Forever
Defined clear, flap card base
and insert and ribbon: Making Memories
Embossing texture plate: EK Success
Flower: Savvy Stamper

Friendship Card Set and Box
Defined clear, fabric swatches,
foam stamps, ribbon, scrapbook
colors acrylic paint, tiny alphabets
and washer word: Making Memories
Shipping tag: Avery
Other: Book paper, box lid, chipboard,
fabric, note card envelopes and ribbon

Happy Anniversary
Cardstock tag, charmed phrase,
defined clear, fabric swatches, matchbook
card base and insert and ribbon:
Making Memories
Clip: 7Gypsies
Other: Fabric, felt and ribbon

Card File
Alphabet rub-ons, blossoms, MM kids
trim, ribbon, ribbon attachments,
rub-ons mini and woven ribbon:
Making Memories
Paper: Bazzill Basics
Other: Vellum envelopes

Baby
Flap card base and insert, mini brad,
MM kids fresh stickers, MM kids paper
and MM kids trim: Making Memories
Other: Felt

Baby Girl
Matchbook card base and insert,
mini brad, ribbon and ribbon words:
Making Memories
Other: Flower and hatpin

Adore You
Classic small card base and insert,
mini brads, MM kids trim, rub-ons
wordage, snap and woven ribbon:
Making Memories

Friendship
Alphabet rub-ons, defined clear, gatefold
card base and insert, MM kids paper,
MM kids trim, page pebble, rub-ons mini
and woven ribbon: Making Memories
Metal frame: Li'l Davis Designs
Stamping Ink: Shadow Ink

You Are My Favorite
Avenue embellishment paper, rub-ons
images, rub-ons mini, window card base
and woven ribbon: Making Memories

Love You
Avenue embellishment paper, pocket
card base and insert and ribbon words:
Making Memories
Other: Ribbon

Missing You
Blossom, mini brad, ribbon and tag
with pocket card base and insert:
Making Memories

Thanks
Avenue embellishment paper, cardstock
tag, flap card base, ribbon and rub-ons
mini: Making Memories

Celebrate
Gameboard shape, mini brad, pocket
card base and insert, ribbon, ribbon
charm, ribbon charm alphabets, ribbon
words and scrapbook colors acrylic paint:
Making Memories

Little Man
Artistic tag, defined, gatefold card
base, MM kids paper, MM kids trim,
ribbon, scrapbook colors acrylic paint
and staples: Making Memories
Photo corner: Kolo
Other: Button

Happy Birthday
Bookplate: Li'l Davis Designs
Jelly label, MM kids button, MM kids
paper, ribbon and window card base:
Making Memories

Thanks
Alphabet rub-ons, blossoms, mini
brad, MM kids paper, ribbon, ribbon
words and window card base:
Making Memories

Congrats
Cardstock, MM kids buttons, MM kids
paper, MM kids trim and rub-ons mini:
Making Memories
Other: Felt

Happy Birthday
Flap card base and insert, mini
brads, MM kids paper, ribbon and
rub-ons mini: Making Memories
Other: Felt

Love
Charmed, dyeable trim, matchbook
card base and insert and ribbon:
Making Memories
Computer font: Black Jack downloaded
from the Internet

Thank You
Charmed word, classic card base and
insert, cosmo ribbon, defined clear and
ribbon: Making Memories
Other: Button

For Keeps
Alphabet rub-ons, foam stamps,
gameboard shapes, mini brads,
MM kids trim, ribbon, ribbon words,
rub-ons images and scrapbook colors
acrylic paint: Making Memories

Happy Birthday
Dyeable trim, rub-on images, vintage
hip trim and window card base:
Making Memories
Other: Rhinestones and ribbon

XoXo
Cardstock tags, dyeable trim, staple,
tag with pocket card base and insert
and vintage hip trim: Making Memories
Other: Rhinestone button

CHAPTER 3

Floral Gift Bag (intricate)
Cosmo ribbon, eyelets, MM kids paper,
MM kids trim and monogram:
Making Memories
Other: Rope

Floral Gift Bag (moderate)
MM kids paper, MM kids trim and
petals: Making Memories
Gift bag: Xpedex
Other: Rickrack

Floral Gift Bag (simple)
Mini brads, MM kids paper, MM kids
trim, monogram and ribbon:
Making Memories
Gift bag: Xpedex

Travel Box
Gameboard alphabets, gameboard tags, jigsaw alphabets, metal signage, photo anchors, ribbon, ribbon words, scrapbook colors acrylic paint and staples: Making Memories
Paint: Delta
Other: Metal box and primer

Best Buds Gift Box
Gameboard tag, MM kids trim, page pebble and stitches: Making Memories
Other: Buttons and tissue paper

Happy Birthday Gift Bag
Bead chain, fabric swatch, foam stamps, ribbon attachments, scrapbook colors acrylic paint, tag and woven ribbon: Making Memories
Computer font: Borderzone downloaded from the Internet
T-shirt transfer: Avery
Other: Canvas, clear button, embroidery thread and silk flower

Fabric-Covered Tag
Artisan label, defined clear, eyelet, jump ring and ribbon: Making Memories
Tag: Avery
Other: Charm, corsage pin and fabric

Ribbon Bows Gift Box
Decorative scissors: Fiskars
Vintage hip trim: Making Memories
Other: Crinkled paper and silk

Vintage Tag Set
Blossom, decorative brad, jelly labels, mini brads, MM kids trim, page pebbles, staples, vintage hip trim and woven label: Making Memories
Paper: Bazzill Basics
Other: Paper, ribbon, tin box and vellum

CHAPTER 4

Lotus Flower Candle Votive (simple)
Staples: Making Memories
Other: Candles, glass votives and ribbon

Lotus Flower Candle Votive (moderate)
MM kids trim and staples: Making Memories
Other: Candle, ribbon and votive candle holder

Lotus Flower Candle Votive (intricate)
Staples: Making Memories
Other: Ribbon

Baby Garland
Fabric swatch, fabric tags, foam stamp, gameboard alphabet, metal frames, MM kids trim, ribbon, rub-ons mini, scrapbook colors acrylic paint and vintage hip trim: Making Memories
Curtain clips and rings: Newell Window Furnishings
Other: Buttons, chenille, crystal and ribbon

Hanging Monogram
Decoupage medium: Mod Podge by Plaid Industries
MM kids trim, ribbon, ribbon charm alphabets, scrapbook colors acrylic paint and word fetti: Making Memories
Other: Hoop earring, letter and ribbon

Candle Set
Candles: Pier One Imports
Defined clear, ribbon attachments and woven ribbon: Making Memories

Ribbon Frame
Charmed word, ribbon, rub-ons mini and scrapbook colors acrylic paint: Making Memories
Mini clothes pin: Hirschberg Schutz & Co.
Other: Corner brackets, frame and silk flowers

Flower Lamp
Eyelet charms, ribbon and scrapbook colors acrylic paint: Making Memories
Lamp and shade: Target
Other: Button, fabric and ribbon

Flower Pillow
Eyelet charms, ribbon and scrapbook colors acrylic paint: Making Memories
Pillow: Target
Other: Fabric, rhinestone buttons and ribbon

Shadow Box
Label holder, metal mesh, mini brads, monogram and vintage hip trim: Making Memories
Ribbon: Wrights
Other: Fabric, foam core, frame, pins, silk leaves, vellum and vintage button

Pillow Shams

Pillowcases: Mainstay's Home
Vintage hip trim: Making Memories
Other: Pillow form

Monogram
Cardstock tags, eyelet letter, foam stamp, scrapbook colors acrylic paint, trinket pin and woven ribbon: Making Memories
Letter: Pottery Barn Kids
Other: Charm

Topiary
MM kids trim, ribbon, scrapbook
colors acrylic paint and woven ribbon:
Making Memories
Other: Dowel, florist foam, foam ball,
moss, pins, ribbon and tin pot

Tri-Fold Frame
Acrylic paint: Folk Art
Blossoms, cardstock tag, defined,
eyelet letter, fabric swatch, hinges, jump
ring, label holder, magnetic stamp and
ribbon: Making Memories
Photo corners: Kolo
Other: Antique frames, button,
lace and ribbon

Table Runner
Ribbon and stitches: Making Memories
Other: Fabric and vintage buttons

CHAPTER 5

Happy Baby (intricate)
Alphabet rub-ons, decorative-edged
cardstock, defined clear, dyeable trim,
hinge, label holder, mini brads, photo
anchors, rub-ons mini, rub-ons wordage
and woven label: Making Memories
Die cut: KI Memories
Photo corners: Duck
Punch: EK Success
Ribbon: Offray
Transparency: Hammermill
Other: Rhinestones

Happy Baby (moderate)
Alphabet rub-on, decorative-edged
cardstock, defined clear, dyeable trim,
hinges, rub-ons images, rub-ons mini
and woven label: Making Memories
Die-cut: KI Memories
Flower: Saavy Stamper
Ribbon: Offray
Other: Vellum

Happy Baby (simple)
Alphabet rub-on, decorative-edged
cardstock, defined clear, dyeable trim,
mini brad, photo anchor and rub-ons
images: Making Memories
Date rub-on: Autumn Leaves
Ribbon: Offray

Madison 2004
Computer font: New Zurica
Dyeable trim, mini brads,
paper tags, scrapbook dye
and staples: Making Memories
Spray adhesive: Duro by Manco Inc.
Other: Linen thread and muslin

Shelby
Alphabet charms, blossoms, cardstock,
decorative brads, defined clear, foam
stamp, ribbon charm and scrapbook
colors acrylic paint: Making Memories
Other: Beads, fabric, silk ribbon
and tea bag

Winter Wonderland
Bead chain, eyelet charm, eyelets, mailbox
alphabet, mini brads, photo anchors,
rub-ons mini, sheer frame, snap, tag
and woven ribbon: Making Memories
Computer fonts: AL Uncle Charles down-
loaded from www.twopeasinbucket.com
and Hootie downloaded from the Internet
Elastic: 7Gypsies
Index tab: Avery
Pearl snaps: Prim-Dritz
Other: Chipboard, page protector and ribbon

Solitude
Computer font: AL Eyewitness
by Autumn Leaves
Distressing kit, like it is, MM kids paper,
MM kids trim, ribbon, ribbon charm
alphabets and staples: Making Memories
Other: Tag

Remember When...
Angel wings: Darice
Cameo pin: 7Gypsies
Clock and heart charm: K&Company
Computer font: CBX Watson by Chatterbox
Defined, fabric swatches, jump ring, mini
brads, photo anchors, ribbon charms,
scrapbook colors acrylic paint and
washer word: Making Memories
Spray adhesive: Duro by Manco Inc.
Other: Lace, muslin, old book paper,
petroleum jelly, resin, ribbon, transparency,
velvet, watch crystal and watch parts

Bébé
Fabric swatch, jigsaw alphabets
and scrapbook colors acrylic paint:
Making Memories
Paper: Bazzill Basics
Photography: Melody Averett
Pigment ink: Colorbox
Other: Flowers and ribbon

Family
Blossom, decorative-edged cardstock,
eyelet charm tags, eyelet letter, mini
brads, petite signage, ribbon attachments,
ribbon, rub-ons mini, rub-ons wordage,
scrapbook colors acrylic paint and woven
ribbon: Making Memories

Giggle
Acrylic paint: Delta
Avenue embellishment paper, gameboard
alphabet, gameboard tag, mini brad,
photo anchor, staples, tiny alphabets and
woven ribbon: Making Memories
Ribbon: Li'l Davis Designs
Other: Metal clip, ribbon and tulle

Happy
Button, MM kids trim, rub-ons mini,
scrapbook colors acrylic paint and woven
ribbon: Making Memories

Thanks
Blossoms, ledger paper, magnetic
date stamp, magnetic stamps, MM kids
trim, ribbon, ribbon charm alphabets,
scrapbook colors acrylic paint, staples
and woven ribbon: Making Memories
Embossing powder: Ultra-Thick Embossing
Enamel by Suze Weinberg
Photography: DeAnn Hansen
Stamping ink: Ranger Industries
Walnut ink: Post Modern Design
Other: Buttons and old book paper

Girly Girl
Artistic tag, button, decorative-edged
cardstock, photo anchor, ribbon and
snap: Making Memories
Vellum quote: Autumn Leaves
Ribbon: Bucilla

Moments
Alphabet rub-ons, defined clear, jigsaw
alphabet, league paper, mini brads,
patterned cardstock, petite signage,
photo anchors, ribbon, scrapbook colors
acrylic paint, staple and woven ribbon:
Making Memories
Beads: Art Gems
Computer font: Andale Mono by
Microsoft Word
Transparency: Hammermill
Other: Vellum

Adore You
Decorative-edged cardstock, gameboard
shapes, MM kids trim, patterned cardstock,
rub-ons images, rub-ons mini and rub-
ons wordage: Making Memories
Paper: Lasting Impressions
Other: Ribbon

Sidekick
Computer font: 2Peas Quirky downloaded
from www.twopeasinabucket.com
Avenue embellishment paper, distressing
kit, mini brads, MM kids trim, ribbon and
rub-ons wordage: Making Memories
Ribbon: Michaels
Tag: Creative Imaginations

Girlfriends
Alphabet rub-ons, artistic tag, crystal
brad, decorative-edged cardstock,
gameboard alphabets, gameboard tags,
paper flowers, patterned cardstock and
rub-ons images: Making Memories
Paper: Wild Asparagus
Other: Flower and ribbon

My Daughter
Alphabet rub-ons, decorative brads,
moulding strip, patterned cardstock,
scrapbook colors acrylic paint and
woven label: Making Memories
Paper: Bazzill Basics
Other: Button, hatpin, fabric,
silk flower and tulle

Shades of Chloe
Cardstock, fabric swatch, jigsaw alphabets,
scrapbook colors acrylic paint and stick
pins: Making Memories
Computer font: Yummy Apology
Other: Button, fabric and lace

Springtime
Eyelet letter, jump ring, ribbon and
vintage hip trim: Making Memories
Other: Ribbon

CHAPTER 6

Baby Shower (intricate)
Charmed, MM kids trim, ribbon, ribbon
letter wraps, ribbon words and safety pin:
Making Memories
Frame: Wilton Enterprise
Quote: My Mind's Eye
Other: Baby shoes

Baby Shower (simple)
Eyelet letter, ribbon attachments and
ribbon words: Making Memories
Other: Mini spiral notebook and ribbon

Baby Shower (moderate)
Blocks: The Weathered Door
Computer fonts: Adler and Adine Kirnbrig
downloaded from the Internet
Foam stamps, MM kids trim and scrapbook
colors acrylic paint: Making Memories
Paper: Bazzill Basics
Other: Ribbon

Girls' Day Out
Avenue embellishment paper, dyeable
trim, ribbon, rub-ons mini, staple, tiny
alphabets and woven ribbon:
Making Memories
Other: Hand towel, pillow form,
slippers and washcloth

Spring Brunch

Alphabet rub-ons, blossoms, decorative edged cardstock, eyelet tag shape, mini brads, patterned cardstock, ribbon, rub-ons mini and woven ribbon: Making Memories
Ceramic watering can: Michaels
Other: Napkin and rickrack

Birthday Party

Blossoms, league paper, mini brads ribbon attachments, rub-ons, staples and woven ribbon: Making Memories
Other: Glass, glass jar, glass votive, napkin and tulle

Bridal Shower

Tag: Making Memories
Other: Cards, napkin, ribbon, rickrack, soap and square vase

Princess and the Pea Party

Artisan label, buttons, cardstock, eyelet letter, fabric swatches, jump ring, MM kids trim, ribbon, stick pins, wire and woven ribbon: Making Memories
Beads and elastic cording: Cousin Corporation
Computer font: CK Magnificent by Creating Keepsakes
Decorative scissors: Fiskars
Other: Beads, doily, elastic, felt, flip-flops, gloves, lace, mini silk flowers, ribbon, rhinestones and tag

CHAPTER 7

Art Journal (intricate)

Alphabet rub-ons, eyelets, fabric tape, jigsaw alphabet, mini brads, photo anchors, rub-ons images, rub-ons mini, ribbon and staples: Making Memories
Crayons: Crayola
Mini beads: Provo Craft
Other: Book rings, foam core, ribbon, silk flower and transparency

Sketch Book (moderate)

Alphabet rub-ons, decorative brad, fabric tape and woven ribbon: Making Memories
Sketch book: Moleskine
Other: Pencils and snap

Travel Journal (simple)

Alphabet rub-ons, mini book cover and inner pages and MM kids trim: Making Memories
Paper: Rusty Pickle and Scenic Route
Pen: Sakura

Refrigerator Magnets

Jigsaw alphabets, MM kids trim, moulding corner, ribbon words, rub-ons mini, scrapbook colors acrylic paint and snaps: Making Memories
Magnet strips: Spectrum
Other: Ribbon

Bookmarks

Mini brads, MM kids trim, ribbon charms, vintage hip trim and woven ribbon: Making Memories

First Aid Kit

Dyeable trim, mini brads, ribbon, and woven label: Making Memories
Computer font: American Typewriter downloaded from the Internet
Stamping ink: StazOn by Tsukineko
T-shirt transfer: Epson
Other: Button, oven mitt and resealable snack bags

Baby Gear

Charmed, charmed plaque mini, jump rings, MM kids trim and scrapbook colors acrylic paint: Making Memories
Ribbon: Wrights
Spray paint: American Craft
Other: Basket, bottles, pacifier, rickrack and washcloths

Glass Paper Weight

Blossom, cosmo ribbon, defined mini, label holder, mini brads, MM kids trim and petals: Making Memories
Other: Old book paper and paper weight

Watch and Box Gift Set

Cosmo ribbon, leather flower, ribbon attachments, scrapbook colors acrylic paint, tag and wire: Making Memories
Stamping ink: Stampin' Up!
Toggle clasp: Bead Heaven
Watch face: Geneva by Crystal Innovations
Other: Gift box

CHAPTER 8

Girl's Jeans (intricate)

Jeans: Old Navy
MM kids trim and vintage hip trim: Making Memories
Other: Ribbon and rickrack

Boy's Jeans (moderate)

Jeans: Old Navy
MM kids trim, woven label and woven ribbon: Making Memories
Ribbon: Offray

Girl's Dress (simple)

Dress: Target
MM kids trim and vintage hip trim: Making Memories

Ribbon Watch

Woven ribbon: Making Memories
Other: D-rings, ribbon and watch face

Birthday Tag

Mini brad, MM kids trim, rub-ons mini and tag: Making Memories
Other: Beads, ribbon and wire

Handbag Ribbon Belts

Eyelet tag alphabet, ribbon attachments, ribbon charm alphabets, jump rings and woven ribbon: Making Memories
Other: Lanyard clasps

Woven Watch

Jump rings and ribbon: Making Memories
Other: Chains and watch face

Cosmetic Bag

Woven ribbon: Making Memories
Other: Cosmetic bag, ribbon and tulle

Flower Choker

Leather flowers and ribbon: Making Memories

CHAPTER 9

Flip-Flops (intricate)

Dyeable trim, ribbon and ribbon charm alphabets: Making Memories
Flip-flops: Target
Other: Ribbon and tulle

Flip-Flops (simple)

Buttons and MM kids trim: Making Memories
Flip-flops: Target
Other: Double-sided tape

Flip-Flops (moderate)

Flip-flops: Michaels
Ribbon: Offray
Vintage hip trim: Making Memories
Other: Beading floss, beads and double-sided tape

Memo Board

Cloth push pin modular organization system panel, monogram, push pin, ribbon, ribbon attachments, rub-ons mini, rub-ons wordage and woven ribbon: Making Memories

Bordered Frame

Monogram, scrapbook colors acrylic paint and woven ribbon: Making Memories
Other: Frame, mats, rhinestone buckle and ribbon

Ribbon-Wrapped Container

Ribbon and ribbon charm alphabets: Making Memories
Other: Ribbon and square plastic container

Team Photo Book

Alphabet rub-ons, eyelet charm, eyelet shape, patterned cardstock, ribbon, ribbon label, tag and woven label: Making Memories

Double Frame

Metal frame, metal mesh, mini brad, petite signage, ribbon, ribbon label, word fetti, woven label and woven ribbon: Making Memories
Eyelet screws: Home Depot
Frames: Ikea

Art Project Holder

Decoupage medium: Mod Podge by Plaid Industries
Distressing kit, gameboard alphabets, rub-ons images, scrapbook colors acrylic paint, small magnetic clips and woven ribbon: Making Memories
Other: Wood

Message Center Clip

Alphabet rub-ons, cardstock tag, jump ring and woven ribbon: Making Memories
Clip: Kirkland's

Lip Gloss Lanyard

Crystal brads, eyelet letter, eyelet shape, safety pin, scrapbook colors acrylic paint and woven ribbon: Making Memories
Clip and lip gloss: Bonne Bell
Other: Key ring and ribbon

Bracelet

Ribbon: Making Memories
Pearls: Westrim Crafts

Headbands

Buttons, fabric tape, MM kids trim and stitches: Making Memories
Headbands: Scunci
Other: Double-sided tape, silk flowers and spray adhesive

artists & author

Mellette Berezoski Crosby, Texas

Mellette is a stay-at-home mom and reality-TV junkie who admits that she's a messy scrapbooker but likes to clean up in between projects. When not working on an assignment, you'll most likely find her on her back porch browsing through mail order catalogs, flipping through her old book collection or admiring her flower garden. When it comes to ribbon, striped, dotted, floral, embroidered or any other pattern are her favorites.

Maggie Holmes South Jordan, Utah

Even though she's the mother of three boys, Maggie is all girl. A self-confessed fashionista, she's currently working on expanding her growing collection of purses and bags. Always cheerful, smiling and organized, the one thing she'd have if she were stranded on a desert island would be TiVO. Maggie prefers to store her vast collection of ribbon in glass jars where she can see it and draw inspiration from it for her projects.

Jennifer Jensen Hurricane, Utah

A self-described Coke-only drinker (no diet!), Jennifer is terrified of snakes, mice and heights. But that doesn't stop her from doing the things she loves—trailer camping, cooking and baking, eating eggs for breakfast, exercising and talking on the phone for hours. Jenn adores rayon velvet ribbon and the older it is, the better. She scours thrift and antique shops for her ultimate score—a full bolt of untouched vintage ribbon.

Lynne Montgomery Gilbert, Arizona

Lynne's most recent accomplishment is that she ran in her first 5K race. And she had plenty of time to train since she hasn't watched television in the last five years. She is an avid collector of hair magazines, loves homemade blackberry pie and can hardly buy anything without a coupon. If she had to choose one favorite ribbon, it would be tiny black and white gingham because it goes with just about everything.

Kris Stanger St. George, Utah

To Kris, there's nothing finer than a good pedicure and manicure. Since she's the mother of four, including a newborn, a little pampering is just what she deserves. Other loves include Bath and Body Concentrated Room Spray, planting flowers in the spring, Oprah and the color green in every shade. Her favorite type of ribbon is silk ribbon and her new favorite ribboncraft is creating hair bows for her new baby girl.

Loni Stevens Pleasant Grove, Utah

You'll rarely find Loni without a Diet Dr. Pepper in her hand and good tunes playing in the background. Born on the day Mount St. Helen's erupted in 1980, she's a devoted family gal whose childhood dream was to be a makeup artist/hair stylist to the stars. Loni claims to be totally obsessed with ribbon and saying she has a huge stash of it would be an understatement. Working on this book gave her a chance to actually start using it.

Erin Terrell San Antonio, Texas

Originally from South Carolina, Erin confesses that her least favorite household chore is cleaning up her scrapbook room. She'd much rather be enjoying the spring weather, reading InStyle magazine, grilling outside, traveling or taking landscape photography. Erin often ties daughter Daisy's hair up with ribbon. But it doesn't stay in for long—somehow the ribbons mysteriously turn up as "spiderwebs" all over her house.

Julie Turner Gilbert, Arizona

The Château de l'Isle-Marie in France and the Hotel Del Coronado in California. Just a couple of the interesting places in Julie Turner's "collection" of interesting places to stay. When not traveling to exotic locales, she manages to stay busy home schooling her three children, working on projects and remodeling her house. When it comes to ribbon, she loves experimenting with and perfecting techniques for creating custom embellishments.

Jennifer Kofford AUTHOR Layton, Utah

If there was a sport of extreme bargain shopping, Jennifer just might be the world champion. Getting a great price on anything is a sure adrenaline rush. Among her many loves are traveling anywhere, drinking ice water through a straw, watching movies in a LoveSac and trying on (and occasionally buying) lots of shoes. Because Jen rarely has time to actually craft with ribbon, she is most likely buying, organizing or admiring it.

contributing artists

Wendy Anderson Heber City, Utah

Hillary Bevan Concord, California

Joanna Bolick Fletcher, North Carolina

Charla Campbell Rogerville, Missouri

Janet Hopkins Frisco, Texas

Hosanna Houser New York, New York

Kim McCrary Cedar Hills, Utah

Margie Romney-Aslett Alpine, Utah

Jayme Shepherd Providence, Utah

Robyn Werlich St. George, Utah

be inspired.™